Our Own Coordinates

Poems About Dementia

Edited by Mo Schoenfeld and Annick Yerem

SÍDHE PRESS

Our Own Coordinates
Poems About Dementia
An Anthology

Edited by Mo Schoenfeld and Annick Yerem

Published 2023 by Sidhe Press
https://sidhe-press.eu

Cover Art by Katherine Inglis-Meyer
Logo Art by Aida Vainieri Özkara
Design by Jane Cornwell
www.janecornwell.co.uk

Dedication:

Annick:
For Meme, for Pepe, for all the owls and otters.

Mo:
For my husband, Carl, who moves me deeply every day managing his parents' care.

The cover art by Katherine Inglis-Meyer and the last poem by Bob Long, both of whom are living with dementia, are the two pieces that- for us- hold this book together. The title originates from one of the poems in this anthology, When Sadness is Upon My Mother, by Alison Jones.

Mo Schoenfeld and Annick Yerem

Contents

As if he were Daedalus

Math Jones

Just two scoops of breath to the ailing father.
Dribble up the weight from his chin. Eyes keep
his head from lifting too high; ease them now,
to gather up the wealth of weariness

kept within. Best to let him turn himself,
on the tide, let the jaw-line drop as far
as it can. Come together, will to rise
and impetus of moon - thrown to his feet

and balanced on his bones, takes a frail step:
Son is coming home. Son needs an horizon.
All the pain, bundled in his head as horns,
crunches through, and now he can see the boy

coming in to land wings of feathers and
wax beating heart and sun on their backs

Painting my Mum's Nails

Mims Sully

I wait until she's asleep and her hands are still,
gently curled in her lap, before I turn them over,
place them palm down, fingers spread on her knees.

Lost to me in dreams, she stirs and sighs
as I stroke the brush down each slender, ridged nail
from pink crescent moon to flaking, white-crested tip.

When she wakes, she will lift her hands
in front of her eyes, let them drift and flit,
drowsy as butterflies in a summer breeze.

For hours she'll sit like this, smiling
up at her fingers as they dance. Sometimes,
on good days, they'll alight on my face.

Visiting Hours

Shannon Clem

Today, I am Christina.
And no, I don't remember—
Bouncing on the bed last night;
clanging pots and pans like gongs.

Nor the kitty in the corner
reciting The Lord's Prayer—
Although, that's a funny one.

I want to tell you
talking cats don't exist—
And how much I've missed
your soft dark curls.

They always stuck
on my studs when we'd hug—
But, I've learned not to wear them.

Instead, I tell you
how lovely you smell—
After a bath with dry shampoo—
Feigning modesty for Mrs. Maney
in the bed next door.

My heart shrinks and swells

with each count of the cuckoo.

I rejoice and I mourn you—

Until our faces no longer tell time.

On my way out, through tears,

a man grabs me and says

someone's stolen his wife.

I tell him I am sorry;

peel his weathered hands from me.

And hold them still in mine—

A few seconds more.

The Blanket

Jan Westwood

And sometimes now you disappear
behind the shredded fragments of the past,
your eyes slitted with the effort of remembering
what no longer matters:

the days of appointments, meetings, arrangements
are over,
so too, the hush and dim of the Saturday cinema,
the lovely lights coming up on the stage,
the arc of the ballerinas' arms,
one of us girls rushing in home to you,
frantic to find something lost,
and you telling where it is from your chair
as you sit knitting for a neighbour's new baby.

All gone.
Now memory is melting snow,
there is no road back,
and no path ahead,
there is only now,
this moment,
the squares you are knitting for the carer's blanket,
in case his knees get cold in the night.

The knowing movement of your fingers,

the neat notes of the needles,

steady and strong and intertwining,

the colours and patches of all that has not been lost,

Kindness.

Disintegration

JP Seabright

~~I am~~ unravelling
   piece by piece
layer by layer
   year by year
brick by brick

~~I am~~ uncovering
   roof caved in
windows broken
   bones exposed
foundation shaken

~~I am~~ imploding
   slowly disintegrating
under weight of time
   whim of weather
avoidance of passers-by

~~I am~~ collapsing
   this unreliable mind
dendrites detach
   disconnected silent
an abandoned building

12

Survival Patterns

Alison Lock

From the shore I see white splashes dotting the waters
all around the bay: diving holes, exploding
at intervals, simultaneous, or random. The gannets are plunging.

No preening, no acrobatics, just straight in, their wings
folded tight against their bodies.
They are the hunters, sleek missiles zoned into their prey.

Below the surface, the pilchards scatter. I cannot see
the intricate patterns they weave, or

the kaleidoscopes they forge in their fear.

Alice

Giovanna MacKenna

We are neighbours, she and I,

nine metres and four decades apart.

Connected by a washing line, full or empty;

her sheets swaying are signs of a dry day ahead.

We talk on doorsteps, shout through slatted fences,

pin our wet clothes high together. These brief chats

stretch beyond our mismatched generations, gather

tales of family, history, the commonality of care.

She is eighty-plus, a great-grandmother, a wife,

still. She brushes, wipes, cooks, dusts while

he sits in his glass-walled room and watches

television. They have one each.

Sunk hip-deep in the quicksand of daily tasks,

the work has ground a path through her very brain,

dug deep into the grooves of her possible livings,

held her here, firm, with the labour of tending to others.

She is losing the edges of herself. Fading away

in the wash of a million meals made, floors cleaned,

dirt swept, demands met – she has polished

her character to a slick dull shine, nothing sticks.

He retired at sixty. For her there is no date
to mark the day when she can start receiving.
Her load as daughter, woman, mother-wife
is her whole existence.

She cannot manage he confides, while spectres
of a home that is not his begin to circle.
He is unfussed, the change will not be much,
but she will miss her little freedoms

even if she cannot name them. No more
escapes to butcher shops and bakeries
and coffees with a friend or two
around familiar tables.

In truth, those stopped some time ago when
she began to wander undirected. Her quick
feet blind in streets she used to dance on.
My doorstep now an unfamiliar place.

On rare days, I see her washing flying
under a thunder-grey sky. I watch
it billow and flex beneath the line's constraint,
unsure if it's a signal of surrender or duress.

Untitled Tanka

Anna Orridge

Her fingertips still

brush against that framed photo

of them in Greece, his

hand on her back. Memory

of light, and lightness of touch.

Senryūs

Mo Schoenfeld

hospital wing

in memory of my grandfather, 'Dutch' Campbell

king of one-liners.

old vaudevillian steals spotlight,

bellows reach back row.

hiking past

one small step for man.

sad eyes scan the icy street,

carer's sturdy arm.

Sieve

Ronnie Smith

Dumbfounded, without
a fight. We turned her
home into the Home.
Her garden into safe
walled sitting area.

Shared room, a stranger.
Single bulk-buy wardrobe,
to stare at the unchosen gar
of banal anaglypta. Wheelchair
cleaned in the store room.

Her loneliness grown inward,
constant through long empty days.
Meals alone at a packed table
without the balm of gossip,
less and less time in the group.

The past is today, faces of generations
erased. Blurred visits through failing
eyes, others' memories that stir no love.
A sister long dead, her only company.
Quick kiss and a tear on a cold cheek.

Recall

Kerry Darbishire

I show her photographs
but rivers rise to flood me out
burst the banks of
her bedroom walls.

My mother's pale hands
at the helm of Debussy
keys white as teeth
sweep her away.

Notes rush like lost days
from her upright piano
into the dark night.
Spring   Summer   Autumn

spills across the wood-stained floor
the sound of living   drowning out
the rise and fall
of recall.

Notes on aphasia

Annick Yerem

I used to climb hills with my husband,

freckled and strong, binoculars at the ready.

Look, I'd say:

Mauerläufer. Schneefink. Tannenhäher.

I used to take boats to small islands,

my weary heart skipping a beat

when seals swam beside us,

cliffs came alive under my watchful eye.

Look, I'd say to my daughter

I'll give you names to describe the world.

Use them wisely, protect what you name:

Puffin. Chiffchaff. Stonechat.

I used to walk through woods

always a rucksack, a bar of chocolate

an apple to clean my teeth

Look! I'd say to my friends:

Rouge gorge. Mésange bleu. Pinson des arbres.

There are pathways in my brain
where I hear these birds. I know
their names, the spell to make them
real, but when I speak, they leave one by one,
relics of words, whispers, no language strong
enough to hold them.

Look, I say. A bird. *Beautiful.*

Your words

Sarah Connor

Silver as fish, glinting and dancing,

darting, shimmering, weaving

poured out so generously

spilling from your hands,

like flames, like birds, like leaves,

that's how your words are.

Swift as fish, slipping

just out of reach, your fingers

closing on the last of them,

the smallest, slowest, or on something

strange – a coin, a stone –

that's how they are.

Like fish,

too fast

your hand

too slow

that's how they are

Those things.

They are.

Senryū

Elizabeth Moura

a shadowless life

mother tries to brush the hair

of her reflection

I Want to Speak Please

Alun Kirby

Peter.

And Rita.

'We've all got minds

And we've all got voices.'

Elaine, smoky laugh.

Eric, sidekick, sits stoic.

Maria-Elena,

Tiniest dancer, trailing glorious flames of anger,

'It's not contagious.'

Barbara, all woollen check

Coat, and Colin, over her shoulder.

'We're still human beings.'

'Clinicians put us in our coffins.'

They know, Bob and Sue,

'Dementia is cruel.'

'Once you're diagnosed, nobody bothers with you.'

Wendy, double doctor, double author, tandem skydiver,

'Just let me try.'

Eddy, lifesaver, 'I'm normal inside.'

Alice, wild child, wild horse rider,

And Brian, beside her,

Cap wearer, straight talker, justified curser,

'I'm frustrated.'

'Bad days are lonely.'

There's Ron, she's Sheila, and over there, Penny,

'Never be ashamed.'

'Yes, we're still human beings.'

And Monica, Robin and Glenice,

'I'm me.'

This poem is inspired by collaborating with Minds & Voices, a group of inspirational people living with dementia, over the last few years. All the quotes in the poem are theirs.

Phone calls to my mother

Matt Quinn

First lockdown, 2020

I phone my mother. They have not slept well,
my father up at four, and then at six,
clapping and singing in the conservatory.

Each day the siblings' WhatsApp group reports
the latest news from phone calls to my mother:
My father leaves the house unnoticed, but

he knocks a neighbour's door, who phones my mother.
He puts her trousers on, won't take them off.
He throws a tantrum. He throws other things.

I phone my mother. Not the best of days.
This morning he's afraid of who's outside,
gets anxious if she goes into the garden.

Today in WhatsApp news: the singing group
restarts on Zoom. My father sings along.
We parcel out the times to phone my mother.

I phone my mother, but my father answers,

is baffled when I greet him. *I'm not Dad,*

he says. I ask him if his wife is there.

There's silence, then my mother on the phone.

Bedside

Helen J. Aitken

Jumbled, like her thoughts

A drawer full of memories

We're in there, somewhere

Wellsprings Care Home

Mims Sully

I don't mean to frighten you but I know the building,
it's peculiar, lots of dead ends and walls that move.
Turn a corner and you're locked out. You have to drop
an iron on the gatekeeper's foot to make sure he's still alive.

There's been a fire. We were trapped inside the showers
listening for the alarms that never came, they never come.
There's been a theft. Nobody left until the culprit was found
in a cupboard; turned inside out to see where they were hiding.

The trouble is they give everyone medicine to calm down.
You have to know where you're going or you'll capsize,
shrink into water, wake up in America. And that's why
I'm getting out. If anyone asks, just say I'm with you.

Tracing Footsteps

Susan Richardson

Each morning in the care home,

a nurse dressed my father

in loose-fitting jeans,

a tee shirt, under a button-down shirt,

under a tweed jacket he bought in 1963.

As a finishing flourish,

he insisted on a favourite belt,

worn brown leather punctured with new holes

to fit his shrinking waist.

After the daily ritual of dressing,

he was ushered to a breakfast he never ate,

then set free to roam.

Most afternoons,

I knew he could be found pacing the halls,

searching for an escape hatch.

We walked together,

checking the same locked doors,

looking for secret passageways.

He was notorious for setting off alarms.

Every Friday, he could be cajoled from his wandering

by the promise of ice cream and music.

A piano player came each week,

explored the keys with enthusiasm,

sang Bob Dylan songs.

My father provided accompaniment

with a harmonica he had played as a young father,

and his still beautiful singing voice.

He never forgot the words.

When the ice cream dishes were emptied

and the sounds of music drifted away,

he returned to his search,

tracing footsteps through hallways

that never became familiar.

As we walked arm in arm,

he would ask me,

when are we going home?

I answered him gently,

thirty minutes

right after lunch

soon, I promise.

The Visit

Zoë Green

In our house in the village where nobody locks,

she hides her handbag under jumpers in case

somebody steals it, despite its containing none

of the local currency she forgot to buy.

In a gallery we admire a rock wrapped up

in rope by this artist, Su-Mei Tse. It reminds me

of her, this rock for caving in skulls. Sorry, but

this new silence of hers is black, fatal as a

meteorite. Remember how she used to demonstrate

controlled use of ferric acid to dissolve fields

of copper plate, a technique rarely used in self-

portraiture? Well now, Mum, you've gone too far.

When, waving from the window of the train back north,

she trips and smiles a smile like a wisp of smoke –

it's the first time and the last. Snow spluitters[1] from the tracks;

she's a hundred metres off, then a thousand miles.

_____

1   *Spluitter*: Scots for 'splatter' or 'spray'

She said, quite calm, before she left, she never would

come back. This said to be cruel. So tell me,

where is it you've gone to instead? She leaves her facecloth,

curled around a dripping tap, blue and stiff and dead.

On the third stroke

Ivor Daniel

My Dad's first stroke. Midnight Drama Sleepwalk.
Lady Macbeth not making sense, in Scottish, Welsh or English.
You get in the wrong bed. I have never seen you off your head.

My older brother builds a bonfire to burn a pile of your stuff
from garage, yard and shed.
Indecent haste. (Important men have little time to waste).
He gives my daughter a match to throw on the petrol pyre.
Who am I to judge? (He nearly sets her on fire).

My Dad's second stroke.
We call an ambulance. They know what to do.

Later on, you say to me, 'someone said old age isn't so bad,
when you consider the alternative — but it is, now
and I don't want to be any trouble to anybody.'

'You are not', I say, eyes welling fast enough to fill
a bathtub boat. (How will I stay afloat?)
'We all care about you very much.'

In our family we do not unlearn that it is hard to say
'I love you'
until later.

My Dad's third stroke. Easter. West Wales. Rain.

You had some faith, and now you have some doubt.

You sit there, un-you, as you rest. In imperfect peace.

Somewhere between the Cross and the Crem.

And then you are okay again.

I help you up, and onto the bed.

My younger brother brings clean pyjamas.

Mum kisses you.

We are all getting better at this.

Note: My Dad's three mild strokes marked the beginning of his gradual cognitive decline, over a period of 6 years. Dad passed away in his own bed (in November 2012), after eating Sunday lunch, the day after his sister Rhona passed. R.I.P. Owen Daniel & Rhona Tremaine.

The Language of Flowers

Theresa Donnelly

Abyssinia brings him breakfast on a bamboo tray.

Spoon-feeds him soft-boiled egg;

cuts pale toast into thin soldiers.

Dianthus bathes him in lukewarm water;

massages his often-vacuous head

under a frenzy of melon-scented bubbles.

His scarecrow frame is clad

in chunky wools and heavyweight cords.

Bundled like hay. I push his chair

through institutional doors

into the wash of new light.

His companions are waiting!

Frail fingers reach to touch voluminous heads.

Eyes devour the sapphire delphiniums.

Nostrils fill with the aromatic

scent of French lavender.

Placed in the shade of the wych elm

flora flourish when a surge of long forgotten words

cascade over his tarnished-tongue.

Inexplicably coherent, eloquent,

my father passes the hours in dialogue with flowers.

Until a cold wind stirs the chrysanthemums.

Old bones don't have the appetite for it.

Lady's mantle creeps across

his skeletal shoulders.

Foxglove covers each petrified limb

as baby's breath quietly exhales.

I stand before him

a weed—withering--nameless.

Garthdee

Craig Lithgow

Ah reckon Freda's lookin oot

old photies ae ma Maw,

try'n tae jog Bill's memory.

Or showin him the back pages

o the *Evenin News*

to see whit thur sayin aboot Mitch;

he's been bangin them in

fur Cove lately,

he isnae oot the paper.

But Bill's nae fussed fur the fitba noo,

an even Julie only sparks

a vague flicker o recognition.

He's mair interestet in try'n

tae find his wey back hame.

Just the other week there,

he snuck oot and got on

the Red Line bus towards the toon.

The polis found um doon in Torry,

ootside his childhood home.

Poor auld manny's

been oan lockdoon ever since.

Still, ah'd be willin tae bet

that right noo

he's sittin in the livin room,

in the hoose in Garthdee

- the hoose he's lived in

fur nigh on fifty years -

feelin the gaze o strangers

starin oot at um fae photo frames,

while insistin tae his wife:

It's gittin late Freedz,

ah think we'd best be gawn.

"Mitch" is a local footballing legend who plays for a team called Cove
Rangers. He has a prolific goal scoring record.

Placing a Breakfast Tray Before Florence

Paul Ings

a beaker feeder
and liquids-only resident.

So frail her body is hardly
upon its chair; positioned
along with the careful arrangement
of an array of stone-walled cushions.

Her glowing head is lent back and rests
face upwards at a tilt to the side
experiencing the scene at the window;
the nurse thought that might be nice.

Her expression, of which she has none,
suggests she may have torn free
and is currently become light,
hungerless is weightless, so in flight.

Mild cognitive impairment

Hilary Otto

The carer delivers the day
on a tray with the medicine.
Addled, my mother wakes
tries to persuade her limbs
to change their shape.

It is day. But which?

A wash, a change
from now on each morning
the same effort to stay
the same person until tea
Il y a du sucre?

Oui maman, j'arrive!

The old skills the freshest
you don't read now, you rest
until the carers usher in
the night at half past eight
It is, you comment, *already late.*
Mist blurs the stars tonight.
And so we wait.

The Bookcase In My Head

Roger Hare

is listing to port, or is it

starboard, or sideboard or

am I boring you?

What's important to know

is that my books are slipping

off the shelves, falling - not

onto the floor, just falling.

All the new purchases are going

first, with hardly a chance

to have read them – their gaudy covers

mock my inability

to speak their names.

I can feel the middle shelves

beginning to unsettle their load; all

those busy times we had as a family.

The weightier tomes on the lower shelves

are still there for my reference; the time

I broke Mother's treasured china, our first dog,

the neighbour with outrageous hair, the sneaky look

at one of my brother's dirty magazines.

The Handbag

Debbie Ross

Years ago,

her handbag would have matched her outfit.

Inside, 2 gold metallic lipsticks in shades of pink,

a gold compact with diamanté bow,

Yardley Eau De Toilette,

a neat pack of tissues in a cloth pouch,

some breath mints

and a couple of clip-on earrings

if it had been a late night

and now there's

card receipts folded neatly into a side pocket,

separated from the medicinal insides,

eyedrops, tablets, spare leakproof pants,

a RADAR key

and tissues, new, used, a crumpled serviette,

a purse in a front zipped section

containing no credit cards,

a council ID card

of a self no longer recognised.

Untitled Haiku

Mo Schoenfeld

snow angel, melting,

impatient spring, insistent.

memory fading.

Untitled

Annick Yerem

I walk through the years and past

you flakes of white

bark covering the ground

One day I will wake up

and you will have

snowed upon me

covering what made this

hard what made it

seem unreal

But all of it happened

All of it was true

Act V, Scene IV Of My Mother's Life

Beth Brooke

My mother disintegrates;
little by little she sloughs off her skin,

sheds minute pieces of herself
into the sunlit shafts of spiralling air.

I watch as she dredges through the
sludge of memory for something solid,

something to serve as a handhold
to keep her balanced as she

navigates the slippery path
between one moment and the next.

Her eyes, half-closed, are obscured by
cobwebs; she struggles to focus,

the past too far away, things close to hand
inexplicably unfamiliar.

She is a house unoccupied, dust gathering
in the corners of the cooling rooms.

Nurses' Station, St. Agnes' Ward

Eilín de Paor

Dressed in tidy tweed,

lips a perfect bow, worrying

the clasp of her Sunday handbag,

she paced, restless, waiting

for the next bus into town.

She couldn't tell us who she was late for—

a friend left sitting with a pot for two,

a lover flicking ash under Clerys' clock,

or a shopkeeper, locking up,

pocketing her deposit with a shrug.

I found a chair and Catering brought tea —

we watched together for the driver to skew

through time and space to collect her.

He came while I was off one night.

I passed her stripped bed at the start of my next shift.

He is Gone to the Mountain

Jane Gilheaney

He is gone to the mountain,

and when I want to hear his voice I go there.

It's been a while now,

since his spirit headed home to Miskawn.

To the lay man, he is in Mum's kitchen.

Hands working on something unknown to us.

Words are whispers and his smile holds secrets,

that in good moments light now quiet eyes.

But we know different.

We know, he is gone to the mountain.

Soul returned to Skerahoo.

Blue eyes that are not dimmed at all,

but sparkling in a forest stream,

and gazing warmly into Doon.

The wind on the mountain,

his arms around us,

carries us over the watery earth,

over the winding lane of Potore,

back to the place of his birth.

'Poor Jane' he laughs, walking,

strong as the iron,

lithe as a willow towards Bencroy,

loving the wind that shakes the heather.

The wild a flaming light in him,

too steady to destroy.

I Find Myself

Paul Brookes

How did I find myself here, a spindrift?

Not enough tea in this. It's just water.

Sugar. Can you put more sugar in it?

What's your name? Thank you. That tastes much better.

I need the loo. Can you help me? Always

somebody screams in here. You like my hat?

I need the loo. Where you going? Away?

O, I know her she's nice. Yes, love. Toilet.

She's screaming again. I'm going to lie

down on my bed, love. Will you stay with me?

My clothes no longer fit. They need to buy

me more, that aren't so tight. I like pretty.

Carried coal in on his back. My father.

Water's edge or earth's end? Which is kinder?

Not that type of dementia

Ruth Aylett

Not as in *who am I and where is this?*
but the *I'll sell my flat and move to France* sort.

Not the type where you sit silently
but the one with lots of loud rude remarks.

Not the living on tea, bread and butter version
but the one with pints of port-and-brandy cocktails.

Not *who are you - have we met before?*
but *don't you bloody kids try to tell me what to do.*

Just because we call it Limbo doesn't mean that we don't love you

Marie Little

We pass fear between us
like a chain letter, afraid
not to share it
worried it might bloom like
mould if left alone.
There are days when
we let ourselves think of
other things: the green of
Fairy Liquid, the long
stretch from breakfast until
supper, the shine on a red
apple like a cricket ball
then back round again
we come
telling stories of you
telling your stories
badly, trying
not to tell ourselves
anything.

he who was king

Lynn Valentine

i found the king of my girlhood scattering

the dark in his paisley pyjamas the set

bought that christmas time always hard to

buy presents for that king   he had walked

into night looking for work   for his old

bicycle   thought he could find his way to

the yard   oh king   your hair is snow now

slow come back   come back to the house

oh king   i will take your arm like this

guide you up the steps slow slow oh king

don't you know me   i was once your

princess   i ask again grandfather

don't you know me i will see you safe

to bed this night worry on days and nights

to come   oh king   oh uncrowned king

For Tom and his grandfather

Briony Collins

The last time you saw him, he went for a walk.

Twenty minutes passed before you realised he was gone.

He knew to put on a jumper, because it was October

and the red, reaching light pulled shadows towards each other.

In slippers and silence, he crept away to find his old house,

dragging the slack of his heels along broken, concrete slabs.

You picked him up in the car and brought him home,

just like he did for you today

when his hearse arrived to find you lingering

between memory and fall.

Sylvia

Merril D. Smith

The ocean catches her,

holds her like a jealous lover,

she escapes his grasp--

still, she hears the voice of her true love

in seashell echoes,

in the luring rhythm of ebb and flow,

surf-rush, calling her--

her toes slide into the water,

her ankles—

she pulls one foot out,

the waves caress, draw her back.

Soon she is hip deep in the water,

like a mermaid, she sings,

but only the fish hear her song--

and she is submerged,

swimming toward her beloved.

When Sadness is Upon My Mother

Alison Jones

She lives as a nightmare's shadow,

silhouette gesturing fear,

my hands reach over the gap

between our complicated existence.

I offer meadow fescue, cocksfoot, yorkshire fog,

light gifts pass, hand to hand,

trading homes, meanings, our own coordinates.

I reach for acceptance, tie myself in knots,

try to explain, map the way back.

The grasses rest golden, ripe between our fingers.

asking nothing of us, only that we feel them,

and remember, somewhere coiled in darkness,

echoes of moorlands, birdsong, and deep blue air.

Unravelling

Kathy Miles

His hands are thin as fish-bones,

the fingers webbed and dry.

He stumbles over simple tasks

as he searches for the words he used to say.

At night when the world is dark,

fear swallows him like a whale,

and he is in the heart of it

with a great and terrible question.

I watch him take an hour to eat his egg.

Cracking it open carefully,

hunting inside for the goodness.

She Tells Me

Rachel Handley

She tells me about

miracles coming

through the window. They

arrive amongst the

light to deliver

her from the dead. They

steal from her: Money,

mind. She tells me she

is trapped in a white

room with cakes, and tea,

and no front door. The

man next to her cries.

His question about

where he is, is a

question about why

he is alone. I

tell her we can't go

outside because of

the wind, it would sweep

us

    both

        away.

The Missing Label

Jan Westwood

The label is missing.

The one with your name on it.

The one I ironed on so your dress wouldn't get

lost in the laundry.

The carer brings it to me

And asks if I will iron on a new one.

You are watching us but not understanding.

The fabric is soft in my hand,

I want to hold it to my cheek

like a tenderness which has passed.

The window frames your head.

Beyond, the trees are bonfires,

their leaves fly up like sparks,

ignite the darkening sky.

I sit down, and hold your hand.

We watch together as the dusk envelops

everything and night unfolds like a sigh.

In Summary

Beth Brooke

Things she lost:

days of the week,

the ability to use a telephone,

the route home,

the fact that her husband had

died thirty years ago,

what year it was,

her independence,

how to cook, remember to

eat, the knowledge that

boiling water scalds;

her balance.

Things she lost only sometimes:

our names,

how old we were and where

we were living;

her sense of humour,

earrings,

games of Scrabble.

Things she never lost:

love for my children,

a sense of glamour,

the words to the song, *Are You Lonesome*

Tonight and how to sing it;

the understanding deep inside

that we belonged to her.

THOUGHTFUL REFLECTIONS
for every day...

Bob Long

No! Please don't ask me to reflect

the itinerary.

You can't expect

me to describe

those 'have-been-dones'.

They come and go like moons and suns!

I know I've been in a thoughtful place!

My 'feel-good' holds the warm embrace

that tells me of the moments 'YES!'

My mind still delves for more, not less!

Of course I wish the gift of 'mind'

that seeks its way to keenly find

    the here, the now,

      the way, the why.

I won't 'opt out'!

      I still do try

to find the 'sense' in all I see;

to know again the 'me' of me!

Yet, sad to say, my 'argument' is usually lost.

My 'what?' and 'why?' sent to oblivion.

    my 'oh-I've-got-it!' up and gone!

Then, as usual, let me lie

beside my me and I shall try

my best to rise and shine in light.

But, until then, sweet dreams! Good night x

Biographies

Annick Yerem is a poet and EIC of Sídhe Press. Her book, St. Eisenberg and the Sunshine Bus, was published with Hedgehog Press in 2022. Annick tweets @ missyerem, find out more about her publications here: https://annickyerem.eu and here https://sidhe-press.eu

Mo Schoenfeld has work online and in print, including Irisi magazine, Haiku Crush's Best Haiku Anthology 2021 and 2022 (winning a Judges Grand Mention in 2022), Pure Haiku, The Wombwell Rainbow, Tiny Wren Lit, and the inaugural issue of the Storms Journal. Twitter: @MoSchoenfeld, Mastodon: @MoSchoenfeld@zirk. us.

Katherine Inglis-Meyer (cover art) is a Scottish artist and a former teacher and editor, who now lives in Berlin.

Helen J. Aitken Yorkshire born Northumberland dweller, Helen has spent a career narrating other people's words, whilst quietly penning her own. She has written a collection of children's stories as well as a growing anthology of poems. 'Bedside' was written about her Mum.

Ruth Aylett is an English poet working in Scotland. Her work is widely published, for example in The North, Butcher's Dog, Ink Sweat and tears, Interpreter's House, High Window. Her latest pamphlet, Queen of Infinite Space, is out with Maytree Press. For more see http://www.macs.hw.ac.uk/~ruth/writing.html

Beth Brooke is a retired teacher who lives in Dorset. Her pamphlet, A Landscape With Birds was published by Hedgehog Poetry in 2022. Her pamphlet, Transformations, inspired by the artist Elisabeth Frink, will be published later in 2023. She tweets as @BethBrooke8 and toots as @BethPoet@mastodon.ie

Paul Brookes is a shop asst. writer, and interviewer. Work broadcast on BBC Radio Three, The Verb. Edits The Wombwell Rainbow. Recent work: "As Folktaleteller," (ImpSpired, 2022), "These Random Acts of Wildness," (Glass Head Press, 2023), "Othernesses," (JCStudio Press), 2023.

Shannon Clem is an elusive poet, humorist, & melomaniac rumoured to live with their progeny in California. They have work featured or forthcoming in The Hunger, Versification Zine, warning lines, & elsewhere. Please join them. @shannontantrum

Briony Collins has two books with Broken Sleep – Blame it on Me and All That Glisters – with a third forthcoming in April 2023. She manages her time between running Cape Magazine, working on her PhD, and lecturing

Sarah Connor is a Pushcart and Best of Net nominee, living in North Devon, England, surrounded by mud and apple trees. She has featured in many publications, including Black Bough, Spelt, The Storms. Sarah tweets as @sacosw and posts mostly poetry at https://fmmewritespoems.wordpress.com. She is a regular host at https://dversepoets.com/_

Ivor Daniel lives in Gloucestershire, UK. His poems have appeared in iamb, Fevers of the Mind, Roi Fainéant, Ice Floe Press, The Dawntreader, After..., Alien Buddha, TopTweetTuesday, Black Nore Review, Lit.202, and elsewhere. Twitter: @IvorDaniel   Instagram: ivor.daniel.165

Kerry Darbishire lives in Cumbria. Her poems have appeared in many anthologies and magazines. She has two pamphlets published and her third collection Jardinière was joint winner of the Full Fat Collection published in June 2022 by Hedgehog Press.

Eilín de Paor lives in Dublin and works in services for people with disabilities. Her poems have appeared in *The Stony Thursday Book, Banshee, 14, Abridged* and *Raleigh Review*, among others. Her chapbook, 'In the Jitterfritz of Neon', a collaboration with Damien B. Donnelly, was published by Hedgehog Poetry. @edepaor

Irish/Canadian poet **Theresa Donnelly** has left pencil shavings in places as diverse as Victoria Peak-Hong Kong to the Great Pyramids at Giza. From Singapore to Srinagar-Kashmir. She has two poetry books under her creative belt and is widely published on both sides of the Atlantic.https://twitter.com/TheresaWriter

Jane Gilheaney is an Irish author of dark historical fantasy, poetry and cnf. Her first novel Cailleach~Witch and other writing is available on Amazon. She posts regular writing life updates on her author page at www.facebook.com/janegilheaney

Originally from Montrose, **Zoë Green** lives and works in Vienna and Berlin.

A graduate of Oxford and UEA, her work has been published by The London Magazine, Poetry Review Salzburg, The Interpreter's House, One Hand Clapping, Ink Sweat & Tears, and Atrium. Tweets: @thetrampoet

Rachel Handley is a poet, fiction author, and academic philosopher based in Dublin Ireland. Their poetry has been published by Poetry Ireland and Arlen House, among others. https://rachelhandleywriting.wordpress.com/

Roger Hare lives in Herefordshire, England. He has work in several online and print journals/anthologies, has placed or been short-listed in a few competitions and been Pushcart and Best-of-the-Net nominated in 2021/22. He's on Twitter @ RogerHare6

Paul Ings, born Bournemouth, UK, now lives in the Czech Republic. Poetry in The Reader, Magma, The Interpreter's House, Ink Sweat and Tears, Salzburg Poetry Review, South, etc., and a variety of anthologies. Debut pamphlet *One Week, One Span of Human Life* published by Alien Buddha Press in 2022.

Alison Jones`s work has been widely published in journals such Poetry Ireland Review, Proletarian Poetry, The Interpreter's House, The Green Parent Magazine and The Guardian. Her pamphlets, *Heartwood* (2018) and *Omega* (2020) were published by Indigo Dreams. She is working on a full collection.

Math Jones has performed his poetry widely around the UK. He has a poetry collection, Sabrina Bridge; a poetry novel, The Knotsman; and an album of Heathen verse, eaglespit. Links can be found here: https://linktr.ee/mathjones

Alun Kirby is a British artist now based in Portugal. His artistic exploration of how memory influences our sense of self was recently published in an academic Philosophy journal, and his work is included in 'Pattern and Chaos', to be published by Intellect in 2023 AlunKirby.com @Cyanotype@Zirk.us

Craig Lithgow is an Edinburgh-based writer. Accolades include a highly commended entry to 2022's Edwin Morgan Poetry Award, being invited to exhibit works at this year's Push The Boat Out festival and his poem "Edina Doo" was recently made into a short film by Edinburgh production company, The Scrapyard.

Marie Little lives near fields and writes in the shed. She has poetry featured in: Acumen, Ink Sweat and Tears, Full House Lit Mag, Fevers of the Mind, Anti-Heroin Chic, and more. She also writes poetry for children as Attie Lime. Twitter @ jamsaucer www.marielittlewords.co.uk

Alison Lock's publications include: two short story collections, a novella, several works of poetry including *A Slither of Air* (2011), *Beyond Wings* (2015), *Revealing the Odour of Earth* (2017), Unfurling (2022), and a long poetic sequence Between the Ears: Lure broadcast on BBC Radio 3. www.alisonlock.com Twitter@ alilock4 Instagram@momentsofpoems

Bob Long, an ex Primary School Headteacher has always loved writing in all its forms. He now lives a good life with dementia and enjoys writing as a way of expressing his thoughts and feelings.

Giovanna MacKenna's work has been published by many including Visual Verse, Nine Pens, Abridged and iamb. Her first full collection, How the Heart can Falter, is out now from The Museum of Loss and Renewal Publishing. Go to www. giovannamackenna.com and follow her @giovmacpoet.

Kathy Miles lives in West Wales. Her work has appeared widely in magazines and anthologies, and her fourth full collection, Bone House, was published by Indigo Dreams in 2020.

Elizabeth Moura lives in a converted factory on a river in New England. She has had poetry, flash fiction or photographs published in Human/Kind Journal, Rose Quartz Magazine, The Heron's Nest, Chrysanthemum, Presence, Shamrock, Flash, Flash Fiction Magazine, and other publications. On Twitter @mourapoet, on Instagram at mourathepoet and mourastudio.wordpress.com

Anna Orridge is an English poet and short story writer. She is the winner if the #micropoem21 and Hot Poets competitions. You can find out more about her writing and activism on Twitter (@orridge_anna) or Mastodon (@GreyElm@ mastodon.online)

Hilary Otto is an English poet based in Barcelona. Her work has appeared in *Ink, Sweat and Tears, Black Bough Poetry, The Alchemy Spoon* and *The Blue Nib*, among other publications. She won the 2022 Hastings Book Festival Poetry Competition. Her first pamphlet, *Zoetrope*, is forthcoming with Hedgehog Poetry Press.

Matt Quinn lives in Brighton, England. His poems have appeared or are forthcoming in various places, including Sugar House Review, The Morning Star, Rattle, and The North.

Susan Richardson is an award winning, internationally published poet. She is the author of "Things My Mother Left Behind," from Potter's Grove Press, and "Tiger Lily" an Ekphrastic Collaboration with artist Jane Cornwell, published by JC Studio Press. She also writes the blog, "Stories from the Edge of Blindness."

Debbie Ross lives on a hill in the Scottish Highlands, overlooking the Cromarty Firth. She's been wording since she was wee and has had various poems, articles and short stories published in various places.

JP Seabright is a queer disabled writer living in London. They have two solo pamphlets published and two collaborations, encompassing poetry, prose and experimental work. More info at https://jpseabright.com and via Twitter @ errormessage.

Merril D. Smith lives in southern New Jersey. Her poetry has appeared recently in Black Bough Poetry, Anti-Heroin Chic, The Storms, and Humana Obscura. Her full-length poetry book, River Ghosts was published by Nightingale & Sparrow.

Ronnie Smith is a Scottish born poet now living in southern France. He has been nominated for both the Pushcart Prize and the Best of the Net in 2022 and is presently finalising his first full collection, 'The Largs Poems'. He will be looking for a publisher for this in 2023.

Mims Sully is from Sussex, England. Her publications include Prole, Popshot, Ink, Sweat and Tears and Streetcake. She is currently working on a pamphlet of poems about dementia inspired by her experience of caring for her mother. Twitter:@ MimsSully.

Lynn Valentine lives in the Scottish Highlands. Her debut collection, Life's Stink & Honey, was published by Cinnamon Press in 2022. Lynn has a Scots language pamphlet, A Glimmer o Stars, out with Hedgehog Press (2021). She tweets @ dizzylynn

Jan Westwood is an English poet who lives in Powys, Wales. She was a teacher of English for 42 years and is currently the chair of the Poetry Club at The Poetry Pharmacy. She is also involved in a collaboration between artists and poets in Llanfyllin.

Acknowledgements

A few of these poems have been previously published:

Annick Yerem, Notes on aphasia, Anti-Heroin-Chic, November 2021

Rachel Handley, She Tells Me, https://inkdrinkerspoetry.wordpress.com, Issue 6, June 2022

Alison Lock, Survival Patterns, from her collection Revealing the Odour of Earth, Calder Valley Publishing, 2017

Mims Sully, Painting my Mum's Nails, Visual Verse, Volume 9, Chapter 4, February 2022 https://visualverse.org
Wellsprings Care Home, Strix 7 magazine in July 2019. https://www.strixleeds.com under M J Sully

Eilín de Paor, Nurses` Station, St. Agnes` Ward, Bangor Literary Journal, Issue 13, 2020.

Annick:

To all our contributors: thank you for trusting us with your beautiful work. We are in awe of you.
To Mo Schoenfeld, the best co-editor I could have ever dreamed of, who is also the queen of spreadsheets. I have loved working with you. Let's do it again!
To Katherine Inglis-Meyer for the beautiful cover art. Told you you could do it!
To Alison Jones for the fitting title.
To Aida Vainieri Özkara for the amazing drawing of the Sídhe Press logo.
To Jane Cornwell, for the design and formatting of this book, you are just wonderful.
To Fynn, for all the technical support with Sídhe's website.
To Andreas, my live-in beta-reader, who outdid himself this time.
To Sue Finch for reading the poems with such care and sending us her amazing blurb. We love your work.
To the Flaming Flowers for reading, re-reading and being gorgeous

along the way.
To Peter for his advice and for his friendship.
To everyone who donated a Ko-Fi or more to Sídhe Press.
To Matthew M C Smith for being so generous with his time and expertise.
To Damien B. Donnelly for sharing his editing process and for being who he is.
To Sabine, for putting her trust in me and in this book. It means the world to me.

Mo:

There have been such special, caring, wonderful people involved in putting this project together and those who have been so supportive throughout, and I echo those already thanked by Annick. In addition, I would like to thank my friends Dan Holloway, a great creative mind and friend who encouraged me back into poetry and whose support for fellow creatives is unmatched, and Angelina Schwartz, a fellow writer and college friend who got back in touch during the first lockdown and whose regular video calls with me since then, and support of my work, have helped keep me from despair during difficult times. And, thank you to all I've had the privilege of interacting with in the poetry and writing communities on social media who restore my faith in humanity every time I log in, and all who've connected with and lifted my work in those spaces. I would also like to thank my husband, Carl, for his consistent support and encouragement, as well as our two sons, Max and Oscar, who make my world a far better place than it was before they all were in it. Finally, a huge, teary thanks to Annick Yerem for giving this budding middle-aged poet the opportunity as a guest co-editor on this anthology. It has been pure joy to work with you, and our nearly weekly meetings/chats have been a very bright light as well as among the most fun I've ever had working on a project. Danke Vielmals.

Printed in Great Britain
by Amazon

18757050R00041